KIDS ON THE ROCK!

57 Songs That Help Kids Build Their Lives on the Rock of God's Word

You may make copies of words to the songs in this book if:

❏ you (or someone in your organization) are the original purchaser;

❏ you are using the copies you make for a noncommercial purpose (such as teaching or promoting a ministry) within your church or organization;

❏ you follow the instruction provided in this book.

However, it is illegal for you to make copies if:

❏ you are using the material to promote, advertise or sell a product or service other than for ministry fund-raising;

❏ you are using the material in or on a product for sale;

❏ you or your organization are not the original purchaser of this book.

By following these guidelines you help us keep our products affordable.

Thank you.

Gospel Light

Gospel Light

Living Word Curriculum Division, Gospel Light Publications

Publisher, Billie Baptiste
Senior Consulting Publisher, Dr. Elmer L. Towns
Senior Editor, Gary S. Greig, Ph.D.
Senior Consulting Editor, Wes Haystead, M.S.Ed.
Editors, Lynnette Pennings, Mary Gross
Associate Editor, Linda Mattia
Designer, Carolyn Thomas

WARNING:

The following music may

ATTRACT CHILDREN!

Discretion is advised.
But seriously, folks: This music is different!

Every day, our children are bombarded with musical messages from sources selling products, lifestyles and attitudes that may be contrary to Christian values. We have often tried to attract children to Jesus with music that promotes the very attitudes we don't want to teach—that Christian values are stuffy, old-fashioned, irrelevant and out of touch with today's kids.

FACT: Kids today are much less likely than previous generations to have any background in church music, and are less likely to respond to traditional Sunday School songs.

FACT: Kids are reluctant to sing or listen to anything they perceive as being "babyish," but will eagerly absorb and assimilate music that is popular with older kids.

FACT: Kids think literally. While they easily parrot sophisticated concepts and religious lingo, the mental images and ideas that result may hinder rather than help a child's understanding of God.

CONCLUSION: Today's kids are practically teethed on pop and rock music, whether or not that music is played at home. So they need contemporary, sophisticated-sounding music with words and concepts that are age appropriate.

SOLUTION: The songs in this book communicate God's love and His work in our lives in an effective way: in words kids can understand and rhythms to which they relate.

ONE MORE WARNING:
Adults find these catchy songs irresistible, too!

Good News:

Your musical ability (or lack of it) is not essential to provide good musical experiences for kids!

This songbook has built-in features to help you and the kids become comfortable with new music.

1. Word Charts

Each song in this book has a reproducible word chart for you to use any way you choose. Some ideas:

❑ Make overhead transparencies for your large group to sing along.

❑ On a photocopier with enlarging capacity, copy word charts to fit 11x17-inch paper; place on easel for use with a small group.

❑ Make copies of your group's favorite songs and staple together to make individual "songbooks."

2. Sign Language

Many songs in this book include signs for key words or phrases. The signs used are American Sign Language. Here are some of the benefits:

❑ Kids learn songs more quickly and retain them better when meaningful motions are included.

❑ Actual American Sign Language vocabulary adds an extra dimension to the musical experience by adding another form of communication, rather than simply motions for fun.*

❑ Signing can be a way to draw even reluctant singers into participation in music. And of course, hearing-impaired kids will be delighted that class-mates are learning to communicate in "their" language!

❑ Sign language offers another avenue for expression and interpretation, benefiting both the musical givers and receivers.

3. Simple Accompaniments and Chords

Each song offers several choices for accompaniment. One is sure to suit your capabilities:

❑ Simple keyboard arrangement

❑ Chords for guitar

More Good News:
if you still want more help, it's on the way! Also available are:

1. Reproducible and Split Track Cassettes

Every song in this book can be found on one of the three *Kids on the Rock* cassettes.

❑ Cassettes have reproducible tracks on one side; on the other side are split tracks to use as accompaniment.

❑ Cassettes are referenced by name in the songbook.

❑ You may reproduce cassettes for all the kids in your group to aid learning and build up home libraries of appealing, biblically based music.

2. Music Videos

The first 24 songs from *Kids on the Rock* songbook are featured in exciting new music videos, sung and imaginatively enjoyed by real kids!

❑ Use the videos to learn the suggested signs. In addition to fun you can all sing along with, you and your kids will see the sign language in action for easy learning.

❑ Use them in class. Each song is self-contained, so it's easy to use only the portions of the video you need for your class.

❑ Use them to reinforce Bible truths at home. Your kids can take turns watching the videos at home. (WARNING: Kids will want their own copies!)

❑ Use them to inspire. *Kids on the Rock* videos go far beyond entertainment. The fun and easy creative treatments of each song are designed to spark imaginations. Who knows? You might even want to use some of the ideas to shoot a home-grown video for your own church!

So don't despair and don't delay. You really can enjoy music with your kids—music that will help them remember Bible truths will also make them strong in Christ. Even if you don't have the soul of a musician, your cassette player and VCR can make you more musical than you ever thought you could be! We want your kids—and YOU—to enjoy God's gift of music and to feel successful doing it!

Cassettes and videos are available from your regular Gospel Light supplier.

★ Signs are based on American Sign Language vocabulary taken from *The Joy of Signing* by Lottie L. Riekehof and *The Perigee Visual Dictionary of Signing* by Rod Butterworth and Mickey Flodin.

"So how do i, Ned No-Rhythm Schnockentooter, give my kids a great musical experience?"

We thought you'd never ask!
Just follow these simple guidelines:

1. Learn it.

❑ **Listen to the song** recorded on the cassette, if possible. If you do not have a recording of the song, enlist a friend who reads music to pick out the melody on a keyboard or other instrument. Record your friend's music so you can play it over and over.

❑ **Practice the song** until you can sing it easily and confidently. Learn it well enough to maintain eye contact with kids as you sing, rather than looking constantly at the songbook or word chart.

❑ **Practice any signs or motions** given, using a mirror if necessary, until you can perform them clearly and confidently while singing.

2. Look at it.

❑ **Display the words** where kids can easily see them. Enlarge the reproducible word charts in the songbook or make overhead transparencies so kids can follow along. (An added benefit: Their attention will be focused on the word chart instead of you!)

❑ **Capture interest** before you introduce the song. Connect the song with a subject you've been discussing or mention something to listen for in the song.

❑ **Present the song.** Play the cassette as you sing along. Or, if you use an accompanist instead of the tape, be sure the accompaniment emphasizes the melody line. But whatever you do, do it with enthusiasm! As a rule, kids will adopt your attitude toward a song.

❑ **Discuss** the group's answers to your previous listening assignment. Discuss any words or concepts that might be unfamiliar to the group.

3. Lead it.

❑ **Invite the group to join in singing** a portion of the song, such as the chorus or first verse, as you play the song again.

❑ Demonstrate signs and invite group to join in.

❑ **Sing and sign** the chorus or first verse together. If signs are complicated, divide the group into two and invite one group to sing while the other signs, then switch.

❑ Once you've conquered a small portion of the song, move on to another and repeat the previous steps. Work on a song only as long as kids remain attentive and involved. When interest wanes, move on and come back to the new song at another time.

Contents

The Right Thing

Call and response

God will help us do it, and then it's not so rough!

When we o-bey we do the right thing. When we o-bey we do the right thing. When we o-bey we do the right thing.

2. Saul was the king   (echo)
   Of Israel;   (echo)
   He ignored God   (echo)
   And his kingdom fell.   (echo)
   This made God sad;   (echo)
   Saul couldn't be king.   (echo)
   Saul disobeyed;
      he did the wrong thing.

3. David was   (echo)
   A shepherd boy;   (echo)
   He worshiped God   (echo)
   And sang with joy.   (echo)
   This made God glad;   (echo)
   He made David king.   (echo)
   David obeyed;
      he did the right thing.

Words and Music: Gary Pailer.

The Right Thing

1. Samuel was   *(echo)*
   A man of God;   *(echo)*
   He spoke God's words   *(echo)*
   Strong and loud.   *(echo)*
   He loved God;   *(echo)*
   God was his King;   *(echo)*
   Samuel obeyed; he did the right thing.

Chorus:
Obeying isn't always easy;
Sometimes it can be tough.
But God will help us do it,
And then it's not so rough!

2. Saul was the king   *(echo)*
   Of Israel;   *(echo)*
   He ignored God   *(echo)*
   And his kingdom fell.   *(echo)*
   This made God sad;   *(echo)*
   Saul couldn't be king.   *(echo)*
   Saul disobeyed; he did the wrong thing.

   Chorus

3. David was   *(echo)*
   A shepherd boy;   *(echo)*
   He worshiped God   *(echo)*
   And sang with joy.   *(echo)*
   This made God glad;   *(echo)*
   He made David king.   *(echo)*
   David obeyed; he did the right thing.

   Chorus

When we obey, we do the right thing.

Words and Music: Gary Pailer.

i Know the King

Zydeco

2. David had a giant mess!
   How he'd survive was anyone's guess.
   But David trusted God with everything.
   I'll trust God with my problems;
     He's the King!

3. David had a special friend—
   He was kind to Jon right to the end.
   When I'm with my friends,
     here's what I'm gonna do:
   I'm gonna treat them royally, too!

Words and Music: Judy and Marc Roth.

i Know the King

Chorus:
I know the King personally;
I know the King personally!
(boys) **I'm a prince.**
(girls) **I'm a princess.**
We're royal family.
We know Him personally!

royal
(like a royal sash)

1. God is King over every king.
   He's the Ruler over everything.
   I'm His child, that makes me royalty!
   And royalty is what I'm gonna be!

   Chorus

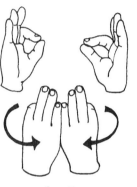

family

2. David had a giant mess!
   How he'd survive was anyone's guess.
   But David trusted God with everything.
   I'll trust God with my problems; He's the King!

   Chorus

3. David had a special friend—
   He was kind to Jon right to the end.
   When I'm with my friends, here's what I'm gonna do:
   I'm gonna treat them royally, too!

   Chorus

Words and Music: Judy and Marc Roth.

Wise Like You

Calypso

On - ly God is al- ways wise,___ but___ a kid can be wise___ some-times.___ I can

do the right thing, do what Je-sus would do.___ Oh, God, help me be wise like You.___ I

want to be smart,___ want to look real-ly swell. I'd like to be fun - ny and draw su-per well.___ And

I want to run fast as the fast-est guys,___ but most of all, Lord, please help me be wise.___

God, help me be wise like You.

Words and Music: Neva Hickerson.

Kids on the Rock 1 cassette

Wise Like You

Chorus:

Only God is always wise,

But a kid can be wise sometimes.

I can do the right thing,

Do what Jesus would do.

Oh, God, help me be wise like You.

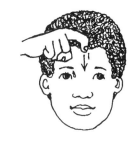

wise
(move finger several times)

I want to be smart,

Want to look really swell.

I'd like to be funny

And draw super well.

And I want to run fast

As the fastest guys,

But most of all, Lord,

Please help me be wise.

Chorus

Words and Music: Neva Hickerson.

Jesus is Born

Appalachian folk style

VERSES:

1. Hal - le - lu - jah to You, Lord Je - sus!

You are born this Christ - mas day.

Hal - le - lu - jah, You are my Sav - ior;

You came to take my sins a - way.

CHORUS:

Hal - le - lu - jah, hal - le - lu - jah, Je - sus is

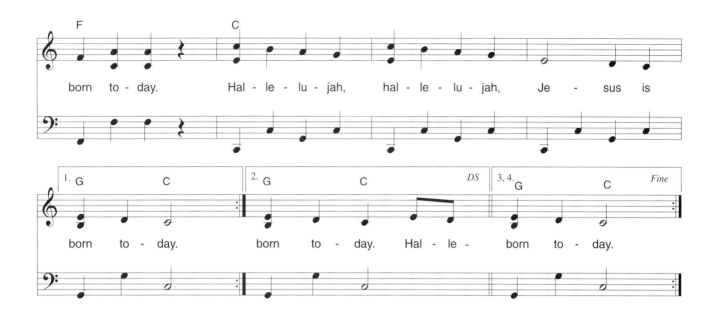

2. Hallelujah to You, Lord Jesus!
   You have come to show the way.
   Hallelujah!
   You came to love us,
   You came to take our sins away.

Words and Music: Steve Luttrell.

Jesus is Born

1. Hallelujah to You, Lord Jesus!

   You are born this Christmas Day.

   Hallelujah, You are my Savior;

   You came to take my sins away.

hallelujah

Chorus:

Hallelujah, hallelujah, Jesus is born today.

Hallelujah, hallelujah, Jesus is born today.

Hallelujah, hallelujah, Jesus is born today.

Hallelujah, hallelujah, Jesus is born today.

Jesus

2. Hallelujah to You, Lord Jesus!

   You have come to show the way.

   Hallelujah!

   You came to love us,

   You came to take our sins away.

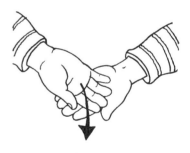

born
("presenting" gesture)

Chorus

Words and Music: Steve Luttrell.

Jesus

Reggae

2. Jesus, You're God's only Son;
   Jesus, You care for me and everyone.
   Jesus, I want to be like You.
   I want You to know,
   Jesus, I'll care for others, too.

3. Jesus, You're God's only Son;
   Jesus, You love me and everyone.
   Jesus, I'm precious to You.
   I want You to know,
   Jesus, I love You, too.

Words and Music: Gary Pailer.

Jesus

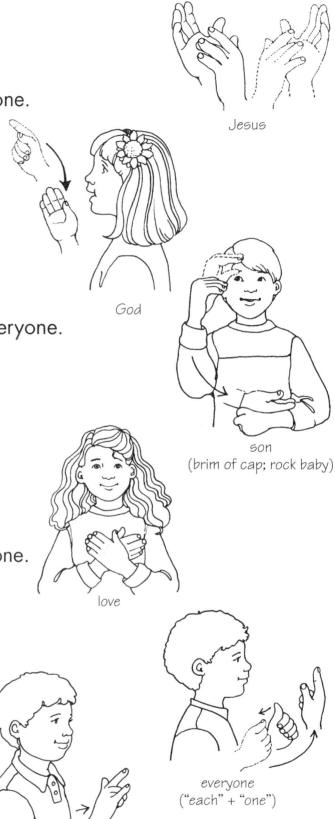

1. Jesus, You're God's only Son;

   Jesus, You love me and everyone.

   Jesus, I'm precious to You.

   I want You to know,

   Jesus, I love You, too.

2. Jesus, You're God's only Son;

   Jesus, You care for me and everyone.

   Jesus, I want to be like You.

   I want You to know,

   Jesus, I'll care for others, too.

3. Jesus, You're God's only Son;

   Jesus, You love me and everyone.

   Jesus, I'm precious to You.

   I want You to know,

   Jesus, I love You, too.

Jesus

God

son
(brim of cap; rock baby)

love

I love you

everyone
("each" + "one")

Words and Music: Gary Pailer.

©1994 Gospel Light. Permission granted to reproduce.

Let Me Say

2. Let me say, "Gracias."
   Let me say, "Gracias, Señor,
   For the good things—
   The very good things—
   You do in my life."

3. Let me say, "I love You."
   Let me say, "I love You, Lord,
   Because You love me;
   You really love me
   Each day of my life."

4. Let me say, "Te amo."
   Let me say, "Te amo, Señor,
   Because You love me;
   You really love me
   Each day of my life."

Encourage children to add "Thank you," "Lord" and "I love you" in other languages.

Words and Music: Neva Hickerson.

Kids on the Rock 1 cassette

Let Me Say

1. Let me say, "Thank You."
   Let me say, "I thank You, Lord,
   For the good things—
   The very good things—
   You do in my life."

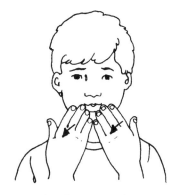

thank you, grácias

2. Let me say, "Gracias."
   Let me say, "Gracias, Señor,
   For the good things—
   The very good things—
   You do in my life."

Lord, Señor

3. Let me say, "I love You."
   Let me say, "I love You, Lord,
   Because You love me;
   You really love me
   Each day of my life."

4. Let me say, "Te amo."
   Let me say, "Te amo, Señor,
   Because You love me;
   You really love me
   Each day of my life."

I love you, te amo

Words and Music: Neva Hickerson.

Easter Round

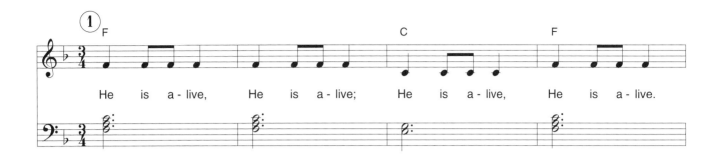

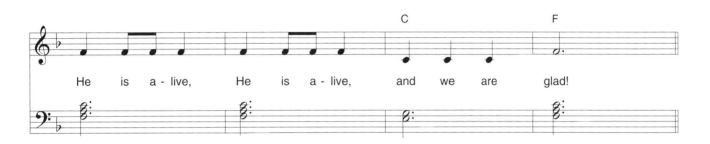

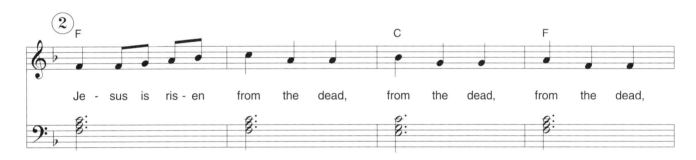

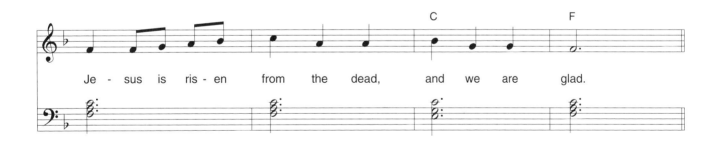

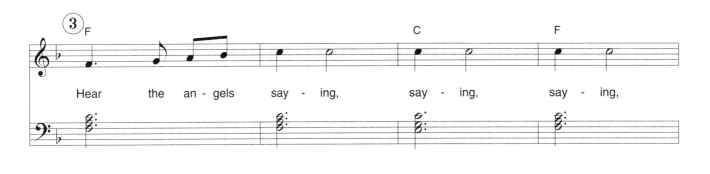

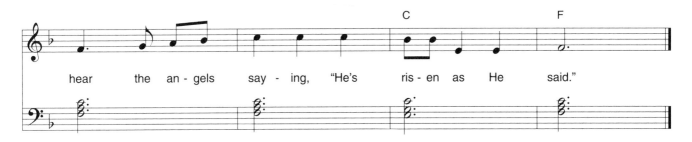

Encourage children to make up their own words to each part of this song.

Easter Round

Part 1:

He is alive, He is alive;

He is alive, He is alive.

He is alive, He is alive,

And we are glad!

Part 2:

Jesus is risen from the dead,

From the dead, from the dead.

Jesus is risen from the dead,

And we are glad!

Part 3:

Hear the angels saying,

Saying, saying,

Hear the angels saying,

"He's risen as He said."

Words and Music: Traditional.

He Looked

Sixties rock

He looked un-til He found me ___ be-cause He loves me so; ___

He's al-ways look-ing out for ___ me; He won't leave me on my ___ own.

God's the lov - ing Shep - herd; ___ He's the per - fect ___ Dad; ___

2nd time to Coda

___ I am im-por-tant to Him; ___ He'll help me through when things look bad.

I'm so glad God loves me, ___ and I'm gon - na let it

Kids on the Rock 1 cassette

show;   I'm gon - na do my best for___ Him,

'cause I want ev - 'ry - one to___ know:

D.S. al Coda 𝄋   𝄌 *Coda*

Words and Music: Mary Gross.

He Looked

He looked until He found me
Because He loves me so;
He's always looking out for me;
He won't leave me on my own.

Chorus:
God's the loving Shepherd;
He's the Perfect Dad.
I am important to Him;
He'll help me through when things look bad.

I'm so glad God loves me,
And I'm gonna let it show;
I'm gonna do my best for Him,
'Cause I want everyone to know:

Chorus

Words and Music: Mary Gross.

Love is What Matters

Calypso

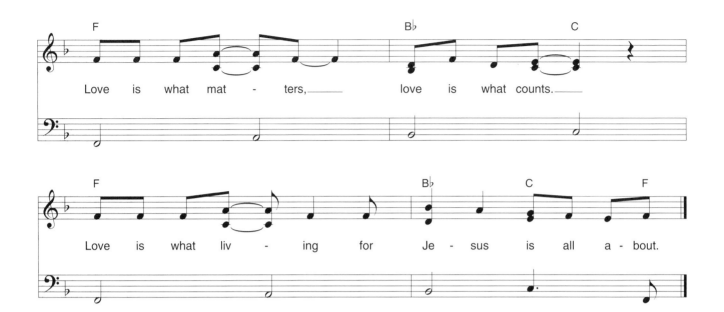

F   B♭   C

Love is what mat - ters,_____ love is what counts._____

F   B♭   C   F

Love is what liv - ing for Je - sus is all a - bout.

2. When your little brother wants to tag along
   Do you tell him, "You don't belong"?
   Or do you remember being his size
   And say, "Today you're one of the guys!"?

3. When you've got a toy that's new
   Do you keep it all for you?
   Or do you share it with someone
   And say, "With you here it's even more fun!"?

Words and Music: Neva Hickerson.

Love is What Matters

Chorus:
Love is what matters, love is what counts.
Love is what living for Jesus is all about.

love

1. When your mom asks you to help clean,
   Do you give her a face that is mean?
   Or do you give her some of your time
   To make those floors and windows shine?

Chorus

2. When your little brother wants to tag along
   Do you tell him, "You don't belong"?
   Or do you remember being his size
   And say, "Today you're one of the guys!"?

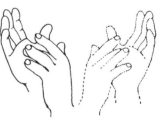
living

Chorus

3. When you've got a toy that's new
   Do you keep it all for you?
   Or do you share it with someone
   And say, "With you here it's even more fun"?

Jesus

Chorus

Words and Music: Neva Hickerson.

God's Holy Book

Bluesy feel

Kids on the Rock 1 **cassette**

God's Holy Book

Chorus:

God's got a plan,

Hold on to His hand,

His Word is true.

God made His plan

Before time began.

God's got a plan for me

And for you.

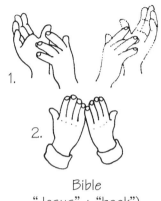

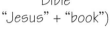

Bible
"Jesus" + "book")

The Bible is God's holy book,

It's God's written Word.

The Bible is God's holy book,

It's the best news ever heard.

The Bible is God's holy book,

It helps us understand.

The Bible is God's holy book,

It tells us about His plan.

Chorus

true

Words and Music: Gary Pailer.

My Perfect Father

Call and response

2. Even when I've done wrong,   *(echo)*
   Even when I'm mad.   *(echo)*
   You'll still be there for me.   *(echo)*
   You're the perfect Dad.   *(echo)*

   I'll ask You to forgive me,   *(echo)*
   I'll trust You with my fears;   *(echo)*
   You know all my secrets;   *(echo)*
   You're the One who hears.   *(echo)*

Words and Music: Mary Gross, Lynnette Pennings.

My Perfect Father

father
(brim of cap + holding up)

1. You're my perfect Father.   (echo)

   You'll never turn away.   (echo)

   You will always hear me.   (echo)

   You listen when I pray.   (echo)

hear, listen

   When I pray, I trust You;   (echo)

   You'll take care of me.   (echo)

   You are God Almighty;   (echo)

   You'll do what's best for me.   (echo)

2. Even when I've done wrong,   (echo)

 pray

   Even when I'm mad.   (echo)

   You'll still be there for me.   (echo)

   You're the perfect Dad.   (echo)

   I'll ask You to forgive me,   (echo)

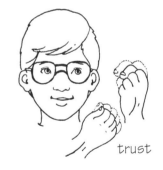

   I'll trust You with my fears;   (echo)

   You know all my secrets;   (echo)

   You're the One who hears.   (echo)

trust

secrets
(sealing
the lips)

forgive

wrong

best

Words and Music: Mary Gross, Lynnette Pennings.

if i Share with You

Bluesy feel

Shuffle (♩ = 104)

Lyrics:

1. If I share with you,_____ will there be an-y left for me?_____ Will I lose my turn___ if I'm___ kind___ as I should be? Will peo-ple___ laugh___ and make fun of___ me? I get scared some - times___ a-bout what's gon-na be,___ but I'm shar-ing___

be-cause I love Je - sus.____

2. When I'd
3. Je - sus

2. When I'd like to keep it,
   I'd like to keep it for myself,
When I want to hide my stuff
   on the back of the shelf,
Jesus, help me remember
   what You want me to do,
You'll take care of me,
   that's why I love You.
And I'm sharing
Because I love Jesus.

3. Jesus doesn't care,
   He doesn't care how much I've got,
And He's good to me,
   He's good so I've got a lot;
But He loves me and
   He wants me to grow;
Sharing's one way I can show
I love Jesus!
Show I love Him by sharing.

Words and Music: Mary Gross.

if i Share with You

1. If I share with you, will there be any left for me?
   Will I lose my turn if I'm kind as I should be?
   Will people laugh and make fun of me?
   I get scared sometimes about what's gonna be.
   But I'm sharing,
   Because I love Jesus.

share
(dividing into two)

2. When I'd like to keep it, I'd like to keep it for myself,
   When I want to hide my stuff on the back of the shelf,
   Jesus, help me remember what You want me to do,
   You'll take care of me, that's why I love You.
   And I'm sharing
   Because I love Jesus.

love

3. Jesus doesn't care, He doesn't care how much I've got,
   And He's good to me, He's good, so I've got a lot;
   But He loves me and He wants me to grow;
   Sharing's one way I can show
   I love Jesus!
   Show I love Him by sharing.

Jesus

Words and Music: Mary Gross.

Promises

Reggae

2. Never again, You promised Noah,
   Would You destroy the world by flood.
   You sealed Your promise
     with a beautiful rainbow;
   Oh God, You always keep Your word.

3. Old Abe and Sarah could have no children
   But You still promised them a son.
   Their children's children like
     the stars in the heavens—
   When You say it, it is done.

4. Sometimes I'm scared of nighttime noises
   And I don't like to be alone,
   But You have said You will be
     with me always;
   Oh God, Your word's strong as stone.

Words and Music: Judy and Marc Roth.

Promises

Chorus:
Promises, You keep Your promises.
Promises, O God, Your word is like rock. *(Repeat)*

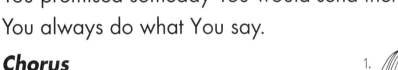

promise

1. Adam and Eve, there in the garden;
   You loved them though they disobeyed.
   You promised someday You would send them a Savior;
   You always do what You say.

   Chorus

Savior

2. Never again, You promised Noah,
   Would You destroy the world by flood.
   You sealed Your promise with a beautiful rainbow;
   Oh God, You always keep Your word.

   Chorus

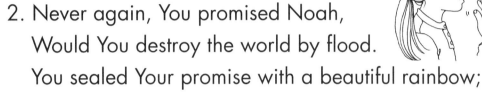

rainbow
("color" + "sky")

3. Old Abe and Sarah could have no children
   But You still promised them a son.
   Their children's children like the stars in the heavens—
   When You say it, it is done.

   Chorus

stars

heavens, sky

4. Sometimes I'm scared of nighttime noises
   And I don't like to be alone,
   But You have said You will be with me always;
   Oh God, Your Word's strong as stone.

   Chorus

with

me

rock, stone

Words and Music: Judy and Marc Roth.

Family Tree

Dixieland

2. The people I live with are all different.
   I can show a little kindness and see:
   When I treat my family with love and respect,
   I can help to grow my family tree!

Words and Music: Mary Gross, Lynnette Pennings.

Family Tree

Chorus:
We all have to live with somebody;
We all have a family tree.
But how we treat the people we live with
Makes a difference in how good it will be.

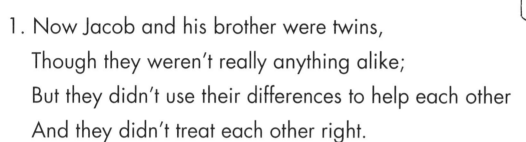

family

1. Now Jacob and his brother were twins,
   Though they weren't really anything alike;
   But they didn't use their differences to help each other
   And they didn't treat each other right.

   Chorus

2. The people I live with are all different.
   I can show a little kindness and see:
   When I treat my family with love and respect,
   I can help to grow my family tree!

   Chorus

tree

   I can help to grow my family tree.
   What a difference—
   How good it will be!

Words and Music: Mary Gross and Lynnette Pennings.

Not Gonna Get Even

Rock

VERSES:

1. There sat Jo-seph in a pit; there was noth-ing he could do!—

When his broth-ers pulled him out and sold— him as a slave, Joe could have

said, "I'll get e-ven with you."— CHORUS: Some-times I'd like to get e-

ven,— some-times it's so hard— to for-give.— Get-ting

e-ven is the thing ev-'ry - bod - y seems to do, but it's not how God wants me to live.

No, God wants me to for - give.

2. There sat Joseph in a prison cell;
   There was nothing he could do!
   As the jail door shut behind him,
   He could have said,
   "I'll get even with you!"

3. There sat Joseph next to Pharaoh's throne;
   Now there was nothing he couldn't do!
   When he had the chance
      to get even with them all,
   He said, "No way! I'll forgive you!"

Words and Music: Mary Gross.

Not Gonna Get Even

1. There sat Joseph in a pit;
   There was nothing he could do!
   When his brothers pulled him out
   And sold him as a slave,
   Joe could have said, "I'll get even with you."

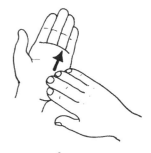

forgive

Chorus:
Sometimes I'd like to get even,
Sometimes it's so hard to forgive.
Getting even is the thing everybody seems to do,
But it's not how God wants me to live.
No, God wants me to forgive!

2. There sat Joseph in a prison cell;
   There was nothing he could do!
   As the jail door shut behind him,
   He could have said, "I'll get even with you!"

   Chorus

3. There sat Joseph next to Pharaoh's throne;
   Now there was nothing he couldn't do!
   When he had the chance to get even with them all,
   He said, "No way! I'll forgive you!"

   Chorus

Words and Music: Mary Gross.

God's Own People

Traditional Hebrew style

VERSES:

1. God's own peo-ple wait-ed man-y years, wait-ed and prayed for Mes - si- ah's birth.

Proph-ets long a-go told this good news: Told that our Sav-ior would come to earth.

CHORUS:

For to us a Child is born, to us a Son is giv- en:

Ev - er- last- ing Fa- ther, Prince of Peace, Won- der- ful Coun- se- lor,

Fine

Might - y God.

2. He has come to earth to shine like light,
   To lead us from darkness and end our night.

   Jesus is the Servant and the King,
   Justice and righteousness He will bring.

Words: Margaret Self, Lynnette Pennings, Mary Gross. Music: Jeanne P. Lawler.

Kids on the Rock 2 cassette

God's Own People

1. God's own people waited many years,
   Waited and prayed for Messiah's birth.
   Prophets long ago told this good news:
   Told that our Savior would come to earth.

   Chorus:
   For to us a Child is born,
   To us a Son is given:
   Everlasting Father, Prince of Peace,
   Wonderful Counselor, Mighty God.

2. He has come to earth to shine like light,
   To lead us from darkness and end our night.
   Jesus is the Servant and the King,
   Justice and righteousness He will bring.

   Chorus

Words: Margaret Self, Lynnette Pennings, Mary Gross. Music: Jeanne P. Lawler

Who is Like You, Lord?

Folk rock

Kids on the Rock 2 cassette

2. I have read the words,
   I have heard the stories,
   How You healed the lame and blind,
   how You quieted the sea.
   I have read the words,
   I have heard the stories,
   How You died and rose again,
   How You saved my life for me.

Second chorus:

(Sing it! Sing it!)
No one's like You, Lord!
(Sing it! Sing it!)
No one's so pure and holy!
(Sing it! Sing it!)
No one is awesome in power!
No one does the things that You do!

Words and Music: Judy and Marc Roth. Chorus based on Exodus 15:11 from the Song of Moses.

Who is Like You, Lord?

1. I have read the words, I have heard the stories,
   How You rescued baby Moses, how You set Your people free.
   I have read the words, I have heard the stories,
   How You led them through the desert,
   How You rolled back the Red Sea.

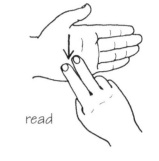

read

   First Chorus:
   (Sing it! Sing it!)
   Who is like You, Lord?
   (Sing it! Sing it!)
   Who is pure and holy?
   (Sing it! Sing it!)
   Who is awesome in power?
   Who can do the things that You do?

heard

2. I have read the words, I have heard the stories,
   How You healed the lame and blind, how You quieted the sea.
   I have read the words, I have heard the stories,
   How You died and rose again,
   How You saved my life for me.

   Second Chorus:
   (Sing it! Sing it!)
   No one's like You, Lord!
   (Sing it! Sing it!)
   No one's so pure and holy!
   (Sing it! Sing it!)
   No one is awesome in power!
   No one does the things that You do!

Words and Music: Judy and Marc Roth. Chorus based on Exodus 15:11 from the Song of Moses.

God is So Strong

Zydeco

2. When I know I've won the race, He's my God.
   When I know I'm in last place, He's my God.
   When I know that I've done wrong, He's my God.
   When I know I can't be strong, He's my God.

Words and Music: Judy and Marc Roth, Lynnette Pennings, Mary Gross.

God is So Strong

1. Stronger than a redwood tree is my God.

   Stronger than earth's gravity is my God.

   Stronger than a hurricane is my God.

   Stronger than a mountain range is my God.

   Chorus:

   He's stronger than you can imagine—

   How can I describe?

   God is so strong, He can make the dead alive!

   He's stronger than you can imagine—

   How can I describe?

   God is so strong, He can make me new inside!

2. When I know I've won the race, He's my God.

   When I know I'm in last place, He's my God.

   When I know that I've done wrong, He's my God.

   When I know I can't be strong, He's my God.

   Chorus

   He's the place where I can hide,

   'Cause His love's so big and wide.

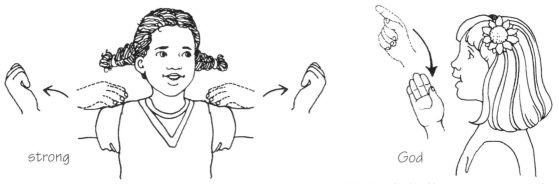

strong   God

Words and Music: Judy and Marc Roth, Lynnette Pennings, Mary Gross.

it's Gonna Be OK

Fifties rock

2. He knows I'm scared of _____ .

   (Shoop, shoop, shoop.)

   He knows I'm good at _____ .

   (Oh yeah ooh wee ooh.)

Words and Music: Neva Hickerson.

***Kids on the Rock 2* cassette**

it's Gonna Be OK

Chorus:

Doo wah ditty

Be bop hey, hey!

He knows me and He loves me

And it's gonna be OK.

1. He knows I like to _____ .

    (He knows me; He loves me!)

    He knows I don't like _____ .

    (He loves me anyway!)

    Chorus

2. He knows I'm scared of _____ .

    (Shoop, shoop, shoop.)

    He knows I'm good at _____ .

    (Oh yeah ooh wee ooh.)

    Chorus

Words and Music: Neva Hickerson.

Easter Means...

Rock

Kids on the Rock 2 cassette

Easter means salvation, salvation means Jesus died for our sins, He rose again, and we'll live forever with Him!

2. Jesus died on the cross one dark day.
   Jesus died for our sins; He is the Way.
   He was buried, He came back to life—
   He rose from the grave!
   This is what we celebrate
   Every Easter Day!

3. Jesus' friends talked to Him on Easter Day;
   Jesus' friends walked with Him
     and talked and prayed.
   Jesus went to heaven,
   Sent His Spirit here to stay.
   We remember Jesus' death
   And resurrection when we say:

Words and Music: Gary Pailer.

Easter Means...

1. People waved palm branches one sunny day;
   People praised Jesus in many ways.
   Some sang songs, some clapped their hands,
   Some shouted words of praise.
   Jesus rode in on a donkey,
   And Easter was on its way.

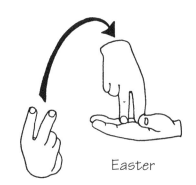
Easter

Chorus:
Easter means salvation,
Salvation means we win!
Easter means salvation,
Salvation means Jesus died for our sins,
He rose again,
And we'll live forever with Him!

salvation

2. Jesus died on the cross one dark day.
   Jesus died for our sins; He is the Way.
   He was buried, He came back to life—
   He rose from the grave!
   This is what we celebrate
   Every Easter Day!

   Chorus

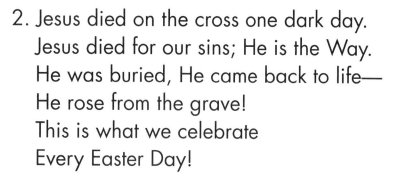
forever

3. Jesus' friends talked to Him on Easter Day;
   Jesus' friends walked with Him and talked and prayed.
   Jesus went to heaven,
   Sent His Spirit here to stay.
   We remember Jesus' death
   And resurrection when we say:

   Chorus

Words and Music: Gary Pailer.

God Loves Every Kid

Reggae feel

God loves ev - 'ry kid, —— there is no doubt.

God's love is the kind—— that leaves no one out, so

when—— you feel—— you don't fit in,—— here's the thing to do. Re -

mem- ber this: God loves me and you!

1. He loves kids with dark brown— skin, — and kids whose skin is light.

He loves kids with lots of friends— and kids who get in fights.

2. He loves kids who run real fast,
   And kids who'd rather sit.
   He loves kids who learn a little slow,
   And kids who catch on quick!

3. He loves kids who need a bath,
   And kids dressed clean and neat.
   He loves kids in fancy homes,
   And kids out on the street.

Words and Music: Neva Hickerson.

God Loves Every Kid

Chorus:

God loves every kid; there is no doubt.

God's love is the kind that leaves no one out,

So when you feel you don't fit in, here's the thing to do.

Remember this: God loves me and you!

1. He loves kids with dark brown skin,
   And kids whose skin is light.
   He loves kids with lots of friends
   And kids who get in fights.

   Chorus

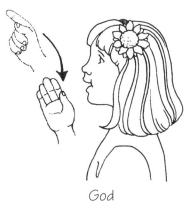

God

2. He loves kids who run real fast,
   And kids who'd rather sit.
   He loves kids who learn a little slow,
   And kids who catch on quick!

3. He loves kids who need a bath,
   And kids dressed clean and neat.
   He loves kids in fancy homes,
   And kids out on the street.

   Chorus

love

kid, child

Words and Music: Neva Hickerson.

Follow the Leader

Rock

Fol - low the lead - er,_____ He shows us what to do._____

Je - sus is our Lead - er;_____ His love is true._____

1. Je - sus died,_____ He rose for me,_____ to

make me part_____ of God's_____ fam - i - ly. When I ask_____ Him_____ and be - lieve,

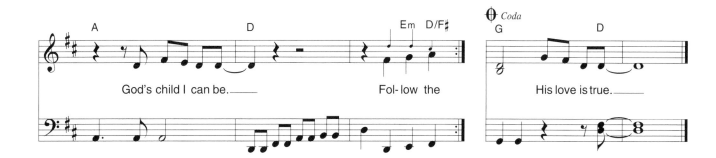

God's child I can be._____

Fol-low the

His love is true._____

2. Jesus knew what to say
When the devil got in His way.
Jesus showed us what to do.
We'll learn God's Word, too.

3. Jesus knew how to pray;
He talked to God His Father ev'ry day.
We can talk to God the same way;
He wants us to pray.

4. Jesus showed us how to share;
He showed God's love
   to people everywhere.
We can tell everyone
Of God's Son.

Words and Music: Judy and Marc Roth, Mary Gross, Lynnette Pennings.

Follow the Leader

Chorus:
Follow the leader,
He shows us what to do.
Jesus is our Leader;
His love is true.

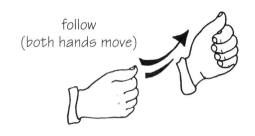
follow
(both hands move)

1. Jesus died; He rose for me,
To make me part of God's family.
When I ask Him and believe,
God's child I can be.

Chorus

leader, boss
(grabbing at clusters
or stars on shoulder.)

2. Jesus knew what to say
When the devil got in His way.
Jesus showed us what to do.
We'll learn God's Word, too.

Chorus

Jesus

3. Jesus knew how to pray;
He talked to God His Father every day.
We can talk to God the same way;
He wants us to pray.

4. Jesus showed us how to share;
He showed God's love to people everywhere.
We can tell everyone
Of God's Son.

Chorus

His love is true.   *(three times)*

love

true

Words and Music: Judy and Marc Roth, Mary Gross, Lynnette Pennings.

Everywhere i Go

Everywhere i Go

Chorus:
Everywhere I go,
With everyone I know,
Even when my life's not fair,
Even when I think no one cares;
No matter what I grow up to be,
No matter who likes me,
I still have Jesus living in me.

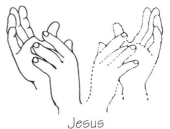

Jesus

1. When I play basketball, He is there with me;
   When I trip and fall, He is there with me;
   No matter what I do, Jesus always is living in me.

Chorus

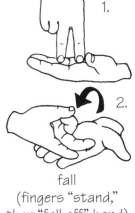

basketball
(shoot imaginary basket)

2. When I'm late for school, He is there with me;
   When I feel like a fool, He is there with me;
   When I feel His care, He is there with me;
   When I forget He's there, He is there with me;
   No matter where I go, Jesus always is living in me.

Chorus

fall
(fingers "stand,"
then "fall off" hand)

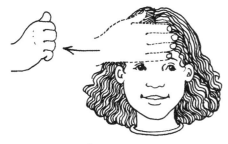

forget

embarrassed (for "like a fool")

school
(two claps)

Words and Music: Marc and Judy Roth, Lynnette Pennings, Mary Gross.

Do What God Wants You To

CHORUS:

Do you want to make the Lord_____ hap - py?__ Do you want to know the best thing to do?_____ Then ya got - ta learn what God wants all His chil - dren to do__ and do what God wants you to._____ 1. There's a

VERSES:

world of__ choic - es right out - side your__ door,__ like should you help your__ moth - er and give mon - ey to the poor? Make the

Kids on the Rock 2 cassette

best choice___ ev - er, choose the right thing to do.___ Yeah,

do what God wants you to!___ Do you

2. Should you smile at the new kid
   And stand up for the weak?
   Should you tell your dad you messed up,
   Should you turn the other cheek?
   Make the best choice ever,
   Choose the right thing to do.
   Yeah, do what God wants you to!

Words and Music: Judy and Marc Roth.

Do What God Wants You To

Chorus:
Do you want to make the Lord happy?
Do you want to know the best thing to do?
Then ya gotta learn what God wants all His children to do
And do what God wants you to.

1. There's a world of choices
   Right outside your door,
   Like should you help your mother
   And give money to the poor?
   Make the best choice ever,
   Choose the right thing to do.
   Yeah, do what God wants you to!

   Chorus

2. Should you smile at the new kid
   And stand up for the weak?
   Should you tell your dad you messed up,
   Should you turn the other cheek?
   Make the best choice ever,
   Choose the right thing to do.
   Yeah, do what God wants you to!

   Chorus

Words and Music: Marc and Judy Roth.

Alleluia

Brightly

Words and Music: Neva Hickerson.

Kids on the Rock: More Songs cassette

Alleluia

Alleluia!   *(3 claps)*

Alleluia!   *(3 claps)*

Alleluia!   *(3 claps)*

I praise You, Lord.

I love You, Jesus.

I love You, Jesus.

I love You, Jesus.

I love You, Lord.

Alleluia!   *(3 claps)*

Alleluia!   *(3 claps)*

Alleluia!   *(3 claps)*

I praise You, Lord.

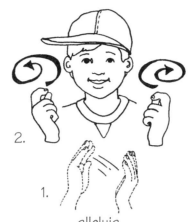

alleluia
(clap once and sign "celebrate")

praise
(two claps up high)

I love you

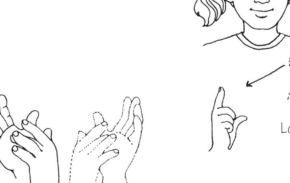

Jesus

Lord

Words and Music: Neva Hickerson.

Be Kind

Traditional sea chantey

Words: Mary Gross, Lynnette Pennings. Chorus: Ephesians 4:32. Music: Traditional.

Be Kind

When I'm feeling angry;   (echo)

When I'm getting mad;   (echo)

When someone else has hurt me,   (echo)

And made me really sad;   (echo)

kind
(as if winding a bandage
around the arm)

I remember something   (echo)

That helps me to be kind.   (echo)

I read it in my Bible;   (echo)

It helps me change my mind.   (echo)

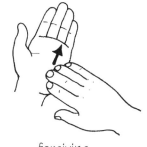

forgiving
(wiping away)

"Be kind and tenderhearted,
Forgiving each other,
Remembering how Jesus
Has forgiven you!"

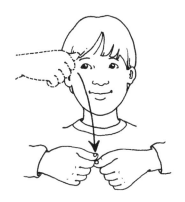

remember, remembering

Words: Mary Gross, Lynnette Pennings. Chorus: Ephesians 4:32. Music: Traditional.

Because You're Good

Traditional

*2. God is so good,

1. Be - cause You're good,_____ be-cause You're mer - ci - ful;_____ be - cause You're

God is so good,

good,_____ O Lord, and mer - ci - ful;_____ I'll trust in

God is so good, He's so

You and I will not be a - fraid, be - cause You're

Kids on the Rock: More Songs **cassette**

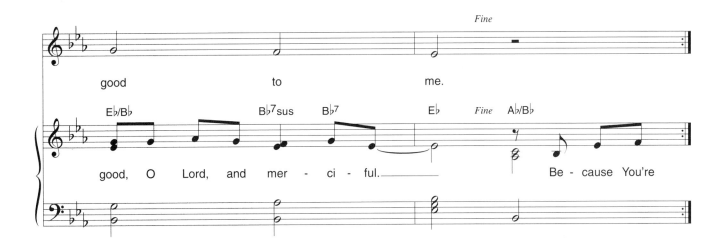

* Sing verse 1 only, then verse 2 only, then sing both songs together.

Words and Music: Traditional.

Because You're Good

1. Because You're good,

   Because You're merciful;

   Because You're good, O Lord,

      and merciful;

   I'll trust in You

      and I will not be afraid,

   Because you're good, O Lord,

      and merciful.

2. God is so good,

   God is so good;

   God is so good,

   He's so good to me.

Words and Music: Traditional.

The Body of Christ

Calypso

1. If *some-one is sad, then ev-'ry-one should feel it, if
*some-one needs help then ev-'ry-one can help (her), If
*some-one is glad, then ev-'ry-one should sing. We're the Bod-y of Christ, each
*some-one needs love, then ev-'ry-one can love.
one can be a mem-ber, and ev-'ry-one can share a part in God's fam-i-ly. 2. If

*Use the name of a child in place of "someone."

Words and Music: David Maddux.

Kids on the Rock: More Songs cassette

The Body of Christ

1. If someone is sad,

   Then everyone should feel it,

   If someone is glad,

   Then everyone should sing.

   Chorus:

   We're the Body of Christ,

   Each one can be a member,

   And everyone can share

   A part in God's family.

2. If someone needs help,

   Then everyone can help (her),

   If someone needs love,

   Then everyone can love.

   Chorus

May use name in place of "someone."

Words and Music: David Maddux.

Christmas Angels

Call and response

2. Jesus Christ has come to earth,   *(echo)*
   Hallelu, Hallelujah!   *(echo)*
   We thank God for Jesus' birth,   *(echo)*
   Glory to God! Peace on earth!
   Good news comes from God to us!   *(echo)*

Divide group into two; have groups sing facing each other.

Words and Music: Mary Gross.

Kids on the Rock: More Songs cassette

Christmas Angels

1. Do you hear the angels singing?   *(echo)*

   Hallelu, Hallelujah!   *(echo)*

   Tell me what good news they're bringing,   *(echo)*

   Glory to God! Peace on earth!

   Good news comes from God to us!   *(echo)*

2. Jesus Christ has come to earth,   *(echo)*

   Hallelu, Hallelujah!   *(echo)*

   We thank God for Jesus' birth,   *(echo)*

   Glory to God! Peace on earth!

   Good news comes from God to us!   *(echo)*

Words and Music: Mary Gross.

Come and Get Together

Rock

Come and get to - geth - er,——— come and praise— the Lord.———

Come and sing His prais - es,——— come and lis - ten to His

Word. Come and get to —

geth - er,——— come and praise— the Lord. Come and sing His

prais - es,——— come and lis - ten to His Word. Come and get to —

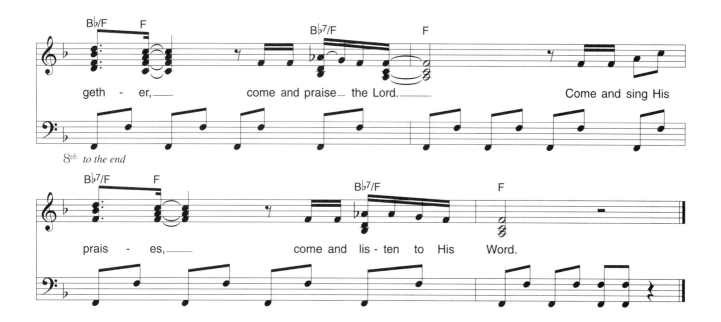

Repeat song as group gathers, singing each verse one step higher than the previous verse.

Words and Music: Bernice Marlo.

Come and Get Together

Come and get together,

Come and praise the Lord.

Come and sing His praises,

Come and listen to His Word.   *(Repeat three times.)*

Words and Music: Bernice Marlo.

Creation Song

Marching song
Call and response

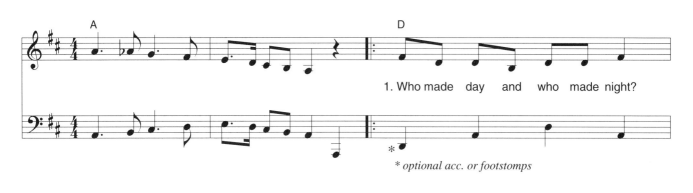

1. Who made day and who made night?

* optional acc. or footstomps

(Who made day and who made night?) Who made all the stars so bright?

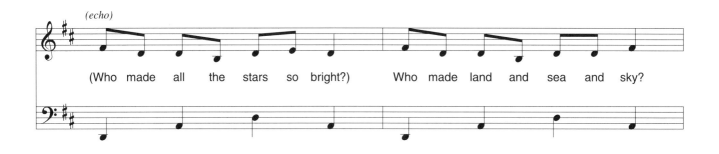

(Who made all the stars so bright?) Who made land and sea and sky?

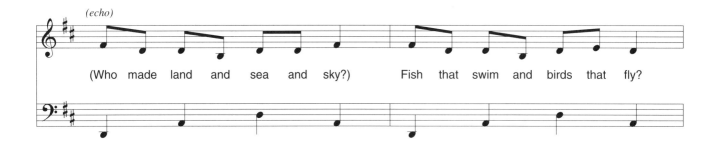

(Who made land and sea and sky?) Fish that swim and birds that fly?

Kids on the Rock: More Songs cassette

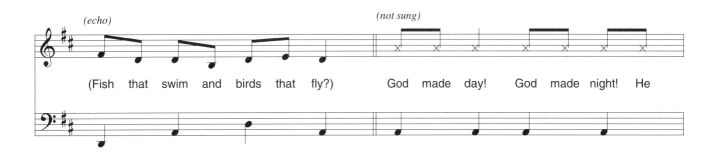

(echo)   *(not sung)*

(Fish that swim and birds that fly?)   God made day! God made night! He

looked at it and said, "ALL RIGHT!"

2. Who made all the plants that grow,
   Leaves above and roots below?
   Who made pine trees tall and green?
   Who made corn and lima beans?
   God made plants, tall and green,
   God made corn and lima beans!

3. Who made bats and bumblebees?
   Flamingoes with their knobby knees?
   Leopard cubs and elephants,
   Wolves that howl and dogs that pant?
   God made made bats! God made bees!
   He made dogs and itchy fleas!

4. Who made people dark and light?
   Gave us earth and sky so bright?
   Who wants us to treat it right?
   Who loves us both day and night?
   God loves us, dark and light!
   He loves us both day and night!

Alternate verses:

Who made dinosaurs and whales?
Things with fins and things with tails?
Jellyfish and sharks and bears?
Things with teeth and things with hair?
God made sharks! God made bears!
Things that make you say, "Beware!"

Who made pigs and lightning bugs?
Mice and moose and slimy slugs?
Who made mold and squirmy worms?
Viruses and tiny germs?
God made bugs! God made slugs!
Things that make you (clap) say, "UGH!"

Encourage children to make up their own verses to this song.

Words: Lynnette Pennings. Music: Traditional.

Creation Song

1. Who made day and who made night?   *(echo)*
   Who made all the stars so bright?   *(echo)*
   Who made land and sea and sky?   *(echo)*
   Fish that swim and birds that fly?   *(echo)*
   God made day! God made night!
   He looked at it and said, "ALL RIGHT!"

2. Who made all the plants that grow,   *(echo)*
   Leaves above and roots below?   *(echo)*
   Who made pine trees tall and green?   *(echo)*
   Who made corn and lima beans?   *(echo)*
   God made plants, tall and green,
   God made corn and lima beans!

3. Who made bats and bumblebees?   *(echo)*
   Flamingoes with their knobby knees?   *(echo)*
   Leopard cubs and elephants,   *(echo)*
   Wolves that howl and dogs that pant?   *(echo)*
   God made made bats! God made bees!
   He made dogs and itchy fleas!

4. Who made people dark and light?   *(echo)*
   Gave us earth and sky so bright?   *(echo)*
   Who wants us to treat it right?   *(echo)*
   Who loves us both day and night?   *(echo)*
   God loves us, dark and light!
   He loves us both day and night!

Words: Lynnette Pennings. Music: Traditional.

God's Family

Mariachi style

I'm a part, you're a part, we're a part of God's fam'-ly, We'll be mak-ers of peace,___ we'll trust our God,___ we'll o-bey His Word. We're glad we're get-ting___ to know our Lord,___ we love to sing praise___ to His name! We're name! 'Cause we're all a part, we're all a part,

of the same fam - 'ly. We're not just cous - ins,___ we're sis - ters and broth - ers,_____ our Fa - ther loves us all.

Words: David Maddux. Music: Mary Gross.

God's Family

I'm a part,

You're a part,

We're a part of God's family.

We'll be makers of peace,

We'll trust our God,

We'll obey His Word.

God

We're glad we're getting to know our Lord,

We love to sing praise to His name!

We're glad we're getting to know our Lord,

We love to sing praise to His name!

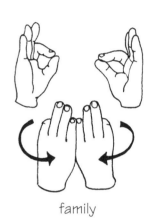

family

'Cause we're all a part,

We're all a part,

Of the same family.

We're not just cousins,

We're sisters and brothers,

Our Father loves us all.

Words: David Maddux. Music: Mary Gross.

God's Word is for Me

Dixieland

2. God's Word (echo)
   Tells about God (echo)
   And His promises to people long ago;
   He still keeps His promises to me, I know.
   God's Word is for me!

3. God's Word (echo)
   Tells of God's love. (echo)
   Sending Jesus is the best gift He gives us;
   Remembering His Word is like
      getting hugs and kisses.
   God's Word is for me!

Words and Music: Mary Gross, Lynnette Pennings.

Kids on the Rock: More Songs cassette

God's Word is for Me

1. God's Word   (echo)

   Helps me to grow   (echo)

   Into the person God wants me to be;

   Helps me to know how much He loves me;

   God's Word is for me!

God's Word
("Jesus" and "book")

2. God's Word   (echo)

   Tells about God   (echo)

   And His promises to people long ago;

   He still keeps His promises to me, I know.

   God's Word is for me!

love, loves

3. God's Word   (echo)

   Tells of God's love.   (echo)

   Sending Jesus is the best gift He gives us;

   Remembering His Word is like

      getting hugs and kisses.

   God's Word is for me!

me

kiss

Jesus

promises

Words and Music: Mary Gross, Lynnette Pennings.

Good News

Good News

Sing it out, sing it out:

Jesus loves you!

Shout the news, shout the news,

Spread the word *(Good news!);*

There are so many people all around us

Who have never, ever heard.

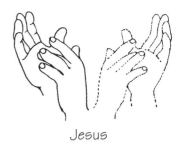

Jesus

They've never heard that Jesus loves them;

They don't even know His name;

They don't know how happy they can be;

They don't know how their lives could change!

So—

Sing it out, sing it out:

Jesus loves you!

Shout the news, shout the news,

Spread the word *(Good news!);*

There are so many people all around us

Who have never, ever heard.

loves

you

Shout the news, shout the news,

Spread the word:

Good news!

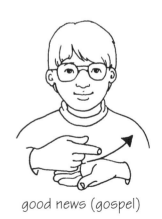

good news (gospel)

Words: David Maddux. Music: Mary Gross.

i'm Gonna Take Care of You

irish jig

Don't let your heart be trou-bled,——— don't let your heart be trou-bled;———

for you trust in God, so trust in Me. Don't trust in Me.

That's what Je-sus said and here's the prom-ise that He made: I'm gon-na take care of you, I'm

gon-na take care of you. Yes, I love you and I'm gon-na take care of you.

Sing the first part faster each time—until your heart is no longer troubled!

Sing the last part more slowly.

Words: David Maddux; based on John 14. Music: Steve Luttrell.

***Kids on the Rock: More Songs* cassette**

i'm Gonna Take Care of You

Don't let your heart be troubled,

Don't let your heart be troubled;

For you trust in God, so trust in Me.   *(Sing three times.)*

That's what Jesus said

And here's the promise that He made:

I'm gonna take care of you,

I'm gonna take care of you.

Yes, I love you and I'm gonna take care of you.

Words: David Maddux; based on John 14. Music: Steve Luttrell.

if i Were a Shepherd

1. If I were a shep - herd and
2. If I saw the old wolf and come
3. Je - sus is our Shep - herd and

had a flock of sheep, I'd take good care of ev - 'ry lit - tle lamb, and
creep - ing through the hay, I'd shake my stick and hol - ler out - loud and
I know He loves me. He helps me grow and shows me how to be what

guard them while they sleep. (Shh!) I'd take good care of
scare the wolf a - way. (Boo!) I'd shake my stick and
He wants me to be. (Yes!) He helps me grow and

ev - 'ry lit - tle lamb, and guard them while they sleep.
hol - ler out - loud and scare that wolf a - way.
shows me how to be what He wants me to be.

Words and Music: David Maddux.

Kids on the Rock: More Songs **cassette**

if i Were a Shepherd

1. If I were a shepherd and had a flock of sheep,

   I'd take good care of every little lamb,

   And guard them while they sleep. *(Shh!)*

   I'd take good care of every little lamb,

   And guard them while they sleep.

shepherd
("sheep" + "person")

2. If I saw the old wolf come creeping through the hay,

   I'd shake my stick and holler out loud

   And scare the wolf away. *(Boo!)*

   I'd shake my stick and holler out loud,

   And scare that wolf away.

sheep
(as if shearing a sheep)

3. Jesus is our Shepherd, and I know He loves me.

   He helps me grow and shows me how to be

   What He wants me to be. *(Yes!)*

   He helps me grow and shows me how to be

   What He wants me to be!

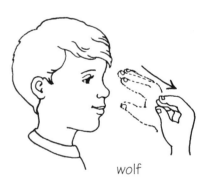

wolf

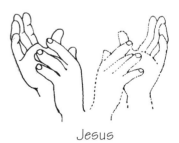

Jesus

Words and Music: David Maddux.

it's a Brand-New Morning

It's a brand-new morn - ing,

time to cel - e - brate and sing! Je - sus is here, and

we're glad He's near, so come on and give a great big cheer!

(Yeah!) It's a brand-new morn - ing!

Words and Music: Neva Hickerson.

it's a Brand-New Morning

It's a brand-new morning,

Time to celebrate and sing!

Jesus is here,

And we're glad He's near,

So come on and give a great big cheer! *(Yeah!)*

It's a brand-new morning!

Words and Music: Neva Hickerson.

Jesus Came to Town

irish hymn tune

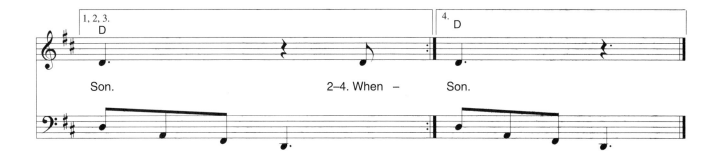

2. Whenever Jesus came to town,
   The kids came for His smile.
   They knew He loved them,
   So they'd sit and listen for a while.

3. Whenever Jesus came to town,
   His friends would come there, too.
   They followed Him and learned from Him;
   That's what I want to do.

Alternate verse:

Whenever Jesus came to town,
He'd tell all those who'd hear
That God the Father loved them all,
That His kingdom now was near.

Words: Mary Gross. Music: St. Columba, modified.

Jesus Came to Town

God's Son, Jesus

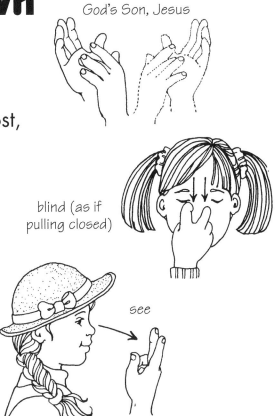

1. Whenever Jesus came to town,
   The hurting people came.
   He knew just where they hurt the most,
   And took away their pain.

   Chorus:
   The blind could see,
   The deaf could hear;
   The lame ones now could run;
   And anyone who'd listen
   Could come to know God's Son.

blind (as if pulling closed)

see

2. Whenever Jesus came to town,
   The kids came for His smile.
   They knew He loved them,
   So they'd sit and listen for a while.

   Chorus

deaf (ear closed)

3. Whenever Jesus came to town,
   His friends would come there, too.
   They followed Him and learned from Him;
   That's what I want to do.

   Chorus

hear, listen

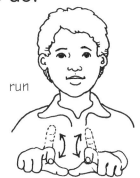

run

lame

Words: Mary Gross. Music: St. Columba, modified.

Jesus Christ is Risen Today

Hymn

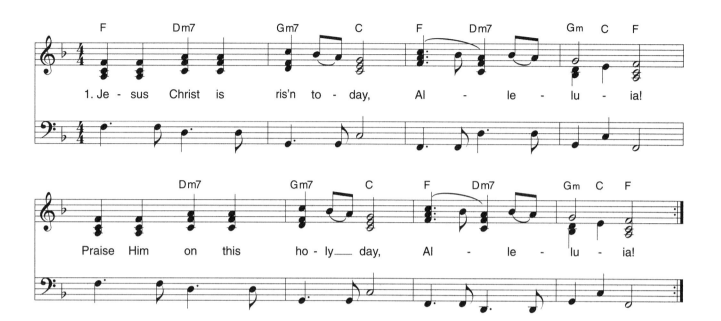

1. Je - sus Christ is ris'n to - day, Al - le - lu - ia!

Praise Him on this ho - ly day, Al - le - lu - ia!

2. Songs of praise now let us sing,
   Alleluia!
   Jesus is our risen King,
   Alleluia!

3. We sing praise to God above,
   Alleluia!
   Praise Him for eternal love,
   Alleluia!

The "alleluias" may be sung as a response.

Words: Charles Wesley, adapted. Music: Robert Williams.

Kids on the Rock: More Songs **cassette**

Jesus Christ is Risen Today

1. Jesus Christ is risen today,

   Alleluia!

   Praise Him on this holy day,

   Alleluia!

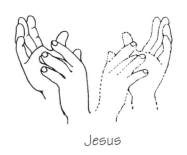

Jesus

2. Songs of praise now let us sing,

   Alleluia!

   Jesus is our risen King,

   Alleluia!

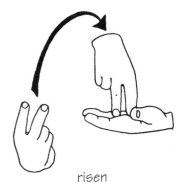

risen

3. We sing praise to God above,

   Alleluia!

   Praise Him for eternal love,

   Alleluia!

Alleluia

Words: Charles Wesley, adapted. Music: Robert Williams.

Jesus Loves Me

Blues
Call and response

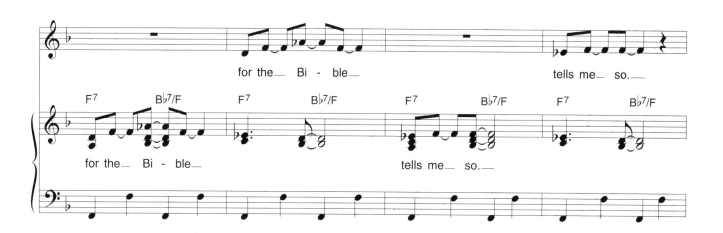

they are weak, but He is strong. He's the

F⁷ B♭⁷/F F⁷ B♭⁷/F F⁷ B♭⁷/F F⁷ B♭⁷/F

they are weak, but He is strong. He's the

Cm/B♭ (Huh!) B♭ 1. F B♭/F

best: J - E - S - U - S!

F⁷ B♭/F 2. F B♭/F F⁷ B♭/F Cm/B♭ (Huh!) B♭

S! He's the best: J - E - S - U -

F B♭/F F⁷ B♭/F F B♭/F F⁷ B♭/F F

S! J - E - S - U - S! J - E - S - U - S!

Words: Anna B. Warner. Music: Unknown.

Jesus Loves Me

Jesus loves me,   (echo)

This I know;   (echo)

For the Bible   (echo)

Tells me so.   (echo)

Little ones   (echo)

To Him belong;   (echo)

They are weak,   (echo)

But He is strong.   (echo)

He's the best:

J-E-S-U-S!

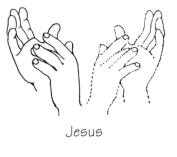

Jesus

loves

me

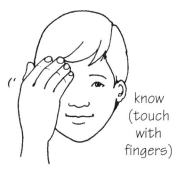

know (touch with fingers)

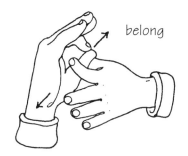

belong

little

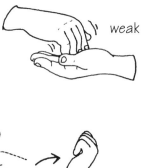

weak

best

strong (shoulders to fists clenched outward)

Words: Anna B. Warner. Music: Unknown.

Let My Words

Let my words and the thoughts of my mind please You, Lord, may they

be the kind that would let all those a - round me see that

I am Yours and_____ You're with me.

Words: From Psalm 19:14. Music: Mary Gross.

Kids on the Rock: More Songs cassette

Let My Words

Let my words

And the thoughts of my mind

Please You, Lord,

May they be the kind

That would let all those

Around me see

That I am Yours

And You're with me.

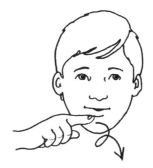

words (finger rolls out)

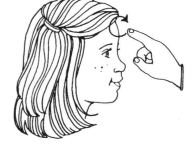

thoughts (finger rolls out)

please
(touching chest)

I

you

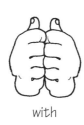

with

me

Words: From Psalm 19:14. Music: Mary Gross.

Lord, i Trust in You

2. Lord, I praise Your name.
   Lord, I praise Your name,
   For You've told me that You love me
   And You never, never change.
   Lord, I praise Your name.

Words and Music: David Maddux.

Kids on the Rock: More Songs cassette

Lord, i Trust in You

1. Lord, I trust in You.

   Lord, I trust in You.

   Let me trust You like

   The people in the Bible used to do.

   Lord, I trust in You.

2. Lord, I praise Your name.

   Lord, I praise Your name,

   For You've told me that You love me

   And You never, never change.

   Lord, I praise Your name.

Words and Music: David Maddux.

The Lord is a Mighty God

Round

❋   *Round begins here second time through.*

X   *Part one of round ends here.*

Words: From Psalm 95:3. Music: David Maddux.

Kids on the Rock: More Songs **cassette**

The Lord is a Mighty God

The Lord is a mighty God

And a mighty King over all the earth.

Oh praise Him, oh praise Him,

The King over all the earth.

Words: From Psalm 95:3. Music: David Maddux.

Love the Lord Your God

Hebrew melody

Love the Lord your God with all your heart;

Love the Lord your God with all your mind; Love the Lord your God with all your strength; O

love the Lord your God.

Words: Deuteronomy 6:5. Music: Traditional Hebrew Melody.

Kids on the Rock: More Songs cassette

Love the Lord Your God

Love the Lord your God

With all your heart;

Love the Lord your God

With all your mind;

Love the Lord your God

With all your strength;

O love the Lord your God.

love

Lord

heart

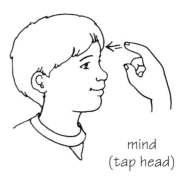
mind
(tap head)

strength

Optional movement steps: Do each movement for the duration of one phrase.

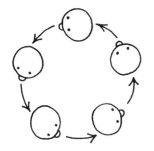

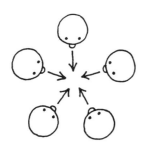

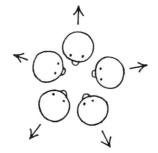

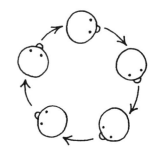

1. Four steps to right (in rhythm with music).

2. Four steps in, then clap over head.

3. Three steps back and clap over head.

4. Four steps to left.

Words: Deuteronomy 6:5. Music: Traditional Hebrew Melody.

Love Your Neighbor

Latin feel

Love your neigh-bor as you love your-self. Spread your love a-round to

some-one else. Keep it hid-den on the shelf.

Love your neigh-bor as you love your self. (2. A) 1. Who's my neigh-bor? Is it

on-ly my friends? Is it on-ly peo-ple that I like? I've

time and love and kind-ness I can spend; I can reach out to a strang-er and find

(shout) (Yes, you should)

(And don't you) (Yes, you should)

Fine

Invite several children to do the speaking part each time.

Words and Music: David Maddux, Steve Luttrell.

Love Your Neighbor

Chorus:
Love your neighbor as you love yourself.
(Yes, you should)
Spread your love around to someone else.
(And don't you)
Keep it hidden on the shelf.
(Yes, you should)
Love your neighbor as you love yourself.

1. Who's my neighbor? Is it only my friends?

   Is it only people that I like?

   I've time and love and kindness I can spend;

   I can reach out to a stranger and find myself a friend.

   Chorus

2. A neighbor is a person who needs someone to care.

   How far can you reach and what can you share?

   Jesus wants us to love people everywhere;

   Love your neighbor as you love yourself.

   Chorus

Words and Music: David Maddux, Steve Luttrell.

Me, Me, Me

you. Then things-'ll be great,___ we can cel - e - brate___ a - bout

us to-geth - er, me and you!___ A-bout us to-geth - er, me and you!

Words and Music: Mary Gross.

Me, Me, Me

1. Give it to me, me, me!
   I want the biggest piece.
   Give me first place in line,
   And things will be fine
   For me, me, me!

me

2. Listen you, you, you!
   You'd better play with me!
   But that's not how to be
   Very good friends
   With you, you, you.

you

   God thinks we're both important,
   God loves both of us the same.
   God thinks we're both important,
   God loves both of us the same.

together

3. What I should do, do, do
   Is be kind and share with you.
   Then things'll be great,
   We can celebrate
   About us together, me and you!
   About us together, me and you!

important

Words and Music: Mary Gross.

My Heavenly Father Cares

Words: Carol M. Dettoni. Music: Traditional.

Kids on the Rock: More Songs cassette

My Heavenly Father Cares

My heavenly Father cares for me.

Wherever I go, He lovingly

Will guide my thoughts and lead my ways.

He cares for me both night and day.

Words: Carol M. Dettoni. Music: Traditional.

Praise the Lord

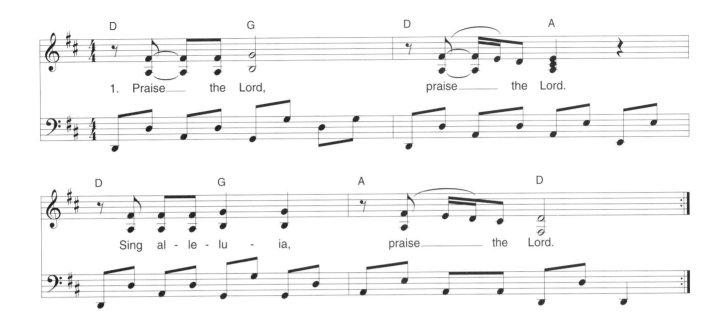

2. He is risen,
   He is risen indeed.
   He is risen,
   He is risen indeed.

3. He is alive,
   He is alive.
   He is alive today,
   He is alive.

Encourage children to make up other stanzas to this song.

Words and Music: Mary Gross.

Kids on the Rock: More Songs cassette

Praise the Lord

1. Praise the Lord,

   Praise the Lord.

   Sing alleluia,

   Praise the Lord.

praise

Lord
(as a royal sash)

2. He is risen,

   He is risen indeed.

   He is risen,

   He is risen indeed.

alleluia

3. He is alive,

   He is alive.

   He is alive today,

   He is alive.

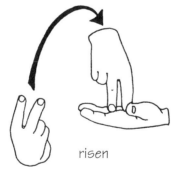

risen

indeed, truly

alive

Words and Music: Mary Gross.

Shalom

Hebrew folk style

Sha - lom, sha - lom, God be with us as we gath-er here to - geth-er, Sha-

lom, sha - lom, God will greet us as we say hel - lo to one an - oth - er.

Sha - lom, friends, sha - lom, wel-come to this place.

Sha - lom, friends, sha - lom, as we meet here face - to - face.

Words and Music: Judy and Marc Roth.

Kids on the Rock: More Songs **cassette**

Shalom

Shalom, shalom, God be with us

As we gather here together.

Shalom, shalom, God will greet us

As we say hello to one another.

Shalom, friends, shalom,

Welcome to this place.

Shalom, friends, shalom,

As we meet here face-to-face.

peace/shalom

hello

welcome

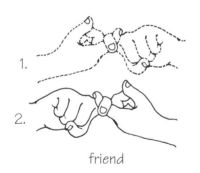

friend

Optional movement steps: Do each movement for the duration of one phrase.

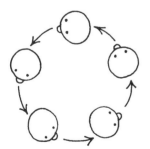

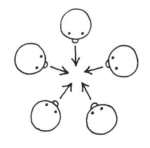

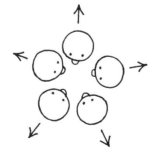

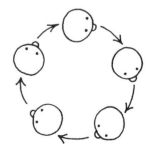

1. Four steps to right (in rhythm with music).

2. Four steps in, then clap over head.

3. Three steps back and clap over head.

4. Four steps to left.

Words and Music: Judy and Marc Roth.

Singing Together

Russian folk melody

Clap hands____ with me and I will clap hands____ with you! (clap)

Clap hands____ with me and I will clap hands____ with you! (clap)

Sing - ing____ to - geth - er, prais - ing God with____ our voic - es,

Sing - ing____ to - geth - er thank - ing Him and____ re - joic - ing.

Clap hands____ with me and we will praise the Lord to - geth - er! (clap)

Words: Carol M. Dettoni. Music: Traditional.

Kids on the Rock: More Songs cassette

Singing Together

Clap hands with me
And I will clap hands with you!   *(clap)*
Clap hands with me
And I will clap hands with you!   *(clap)*

Singing together,
Praising God with our voices;
Singing together,
Thanking Him and rejoicing,

Clap hands with me
And I will clap hands with you!   *(clap)*
Clap hands with me
And I will clap hands with you!   *(clap)*
Clap hands with me
And we will praise the Lord together!   *(clap)*

Words: Carol M. Dettoni. Music: Traditional.

Sorry Song

2. Lord, I need Your help now,
   I'm really feeling angry!
   But I know that's not Your way,
   I know what You're gonna say:
   You'll help me love them anyway,
   Instead of getting even!

3. I don't want to get even.
   I am really sorry!
   I can't forget what Jesus said;
   I'm gonna show love instead.
   I'm feeling bad, my face is red—
   Let's be friends, OK?

Words: Mary Gross, Lynnette Pennings. Music: Traditional.

Kids on the Rock: More Songs cassette

Sorry Song

1. I'm gonna get even!
   You're gonna be sorry!
   I'm so mad I want to kick,
   I'd like to hit you with a stick!
   I better ask for God's help—quick!   *(spoken)*
   Or else I'm gonna get even!

2. Lord, I need Your help now,
   I'm really feeling angry!
   But I know that's not Your way,
   I know what You're gonna say:
   You'll help me love them anyway,   *(spoken)*
   Instead of getting even!

3. I don't want to get even.
   I am really sorry!
   I can't forget what Jesus said;
   I'm gonna show love instead.
   I'm feeling bad, my face is red—   *(spoken)*
   Let's be friends, OK?

Words: Mary Gross, Lynnette Pennings. Music: Tradtional.

Swim Upstream

Boogie-woogie style

Don't be a-fraid__ to swim up - stream,__ to go a-gainst__ the tide;__ just be - cause__ your friends all do it,__ don't go a - long__ for the ride! __ When ev - 'ry - bod — y does it, __ it still does - n't make it__ smart;__ you have__ to live with the things you do, __ and God knows what's in your heart.

E - ven if your friend says he won't be your friend an-y-more;
(she)

say, "That's O. K., I can swim a-gainst the tide; I

won't get left a-lone on the shore, I won't get left a-lone on the shore."

Ev - 'ry-bod - y wants to have lots of friends; we

want our friends to like us too. But Je - sus is my best friend who

knows me through and through, so I want Him to like___ what I do.___

(I) want Him to know___ I'll be true;___

I want Him to like___ what I do.___

Use "she" in place of "he" on the bridge the second time.

Words and Music: Mary Gross.

Swim Upstream

1. Don't be afraid to swim upstream,
   To go against the tide;
   Just because your friends all do it,
   Don't go along for the ride!

2. When everybody does it,
   It still doesn't make it smart;
   You have to live with the things you do,
   And God knows what's in your heart.

Bridge:

Even if your friend says he (she)
Won't be your friend anymore,
Say, "That's OK, I can swim against the tide;
I won't get left alone on the shore,
I won't get left alone on the shore."

3. Everybody wants to have lots of friends;
   We want our friends to like us, too;
   But Jesus is my best Friend
   Who knows me through and through,
   So I want Him to like what I do.

   (Repeat bridge and verse 3 one time.)

   I want Him to know I'll be true;
   I want Him to like what I do.

Words and Music: Mary Gross.

Teach Me Your Ways

Teach me Your ways, — teach me Your ways, — and I'll o - bey You

all of my days. — Teach me Your ways, — teach me Your ways, — and

I will give You praise! praise!

Kids on the Rock: More Songs cassette

Teach Me Your Ways

Teach me Your ways,

Teach me Your ways,

And I'll obey You all of my days.

Teach me Your ways,

Teach me Your ways,

And I will give You praise!   *(Sing twice.)*

teach

obey
(palms face ceiling)

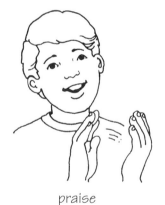

praise

Words and Music: David Maddux.

Tell Only What's True

Rock

1. Tell on-ly what's true, and you won't get con-fused;
you won't have to lie a-gain. You won't have to make up an-
oth-er sil-ly sto-ry to cov-er up what you first said. 'Cause
if you lie, God will know; peo-ple will, too.

You can't take back the words you said; people won't trust you. 2. But it's you. The best thing is telling the truth!

2. But it's good to know
That if you tell a lie
God can forgive you!
If you ask, He'll help you say what's true,
Even when it's hard to do.

Words and Music: Mary Gross.

Tell Only What's True

1. Tell only what's true,

   And you won't get confused;

   You won't have to lie again.

   You won't have to make up another silly story

   To cover up what you first said.

true

Chorus:

'Cause if you lie, God will know;

People will, too.

You can't take back the words you said;

People won't trust you.

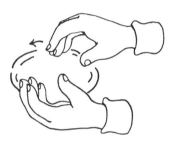

confused (mixed up)

2. But it's good to know

   That if you tell a lie

   God can forgive you!

   If you ask, He'll help you say what's true,

   Even when it's hard to do.

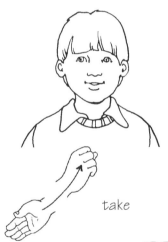

take

Chorus

The best thing is telling the truth!

forgive

lie (across lips)

Words and Music: Mary Gross.

That's What I'm Gonna Do

1. Je- sus loves me so much__ that He died for me,__ His love is with me ev - 'ry day.__

But how can I show__ Him I love Him, too?__ Lord, help me find a way!__

CHORUS:

I can show the kind of kind-ness He showed to me,__ I can

give the kind of love that He gave,__ I can help like He helped,__ and be

Kids on the Rock: More Songs cassette

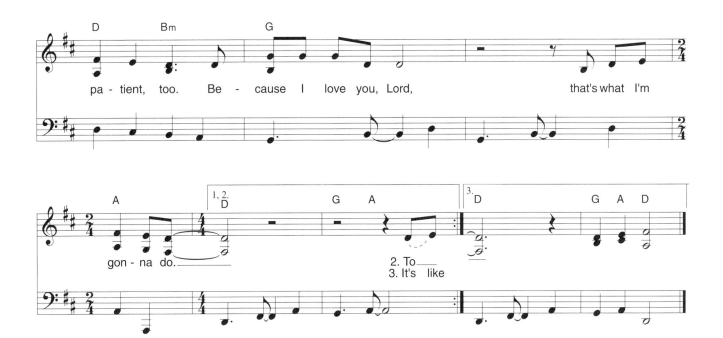

2. To learn to be like Him is a great big job,
   But I don't have to do it alone.
   He will help me each day if I ask Him to,
   Jesus, help me do what You'd do.

3. It's like follow the leader or Simon says,
   I'll read His Word to learn what He did;
   And when I see how He showed
     His love to me,
   I'll show another kid!

Words and Music: Mary Gross, Lynnette Pennings.

That's What i'm Gonna Do

1. Jesus loves me so much that He died for me,
His love is with me every day.
But how can I show Him I love Him, too?
Lord, help me find a way!

kindness

Chorus:
I can show the kind of kindness He showed to me,
I can give the kind of love that He gave,
I can help like He helped,
And be patient, too.
Because I love You, Lord,
That's what I'm gonna do.

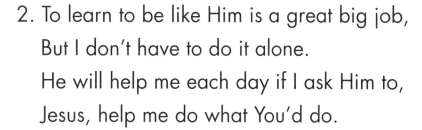

love

2. To learn to be like Him is a great big job,
But I don't have to do it alone.
He will help me each day if I ask Him to,
Jesus, help me do what You'd do.

Chorus

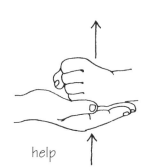

help

3. It's like Follow the Leader or Simon Says,
I'll read His Word to learn what He did;
And when I see how He showed His love to me,
I'll show another kid!

Chorus

patient
(down to chin)

Words and Music: Mary Gross, Lynnette Pennings.

Time to Worship

Reggae

Words and Music: Neva Hickerson.

Kids on the Rock: More Songs cassette

Time to Worship

(Spoken):

Time to stop walkin',

Time to stop talkin',

Time to stop playin',

Time to start sayin'

(Sung):

Time to worship the Lord,

Time to worship the Lord.

Talk to Him, sing to Him,

Time to worship the Lord.

Time to sing to the Lord,

Time to sing to the Lord.

Talk to Him, worship Him,

Time to sing to the Lord,

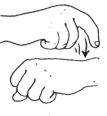

time

worship
(slight shake)

Lord

Words and Music: Neva Hickerson.

You Hear My Heart

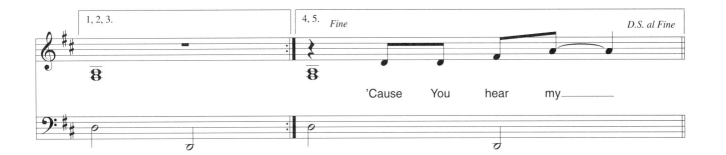

2. Lord, I thank You that when I'm hurt,
   I can cry to You.
   I can ask You for Your help,
   When I don't know what to do.

3. I don't have to talk out loud;
   I know You hear me.
   I don't have to be in a church;
   Don't have to be on my knees.

Words and Music: Anonymous.

You Hear My Heart

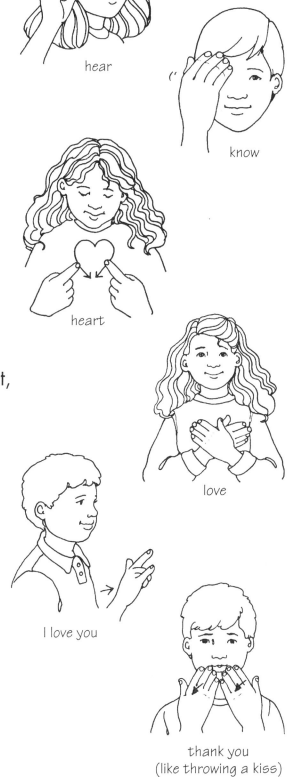

1. Lord, I'm glad I can talk to You;
   'Cause I know You love me!
   Whether things are fine
   And I'm feeling good,
   Or when I'm scared as I can be!

Chorus:
'Cause You hear my heart,
You love me more than I know.
Thank You for loving me;
Lord, I love You!

2. Lord, I thank You that when I'm hurt,
   I can cry to You.
   I can ask You for Your help,
   When I don't know what to do.

   Chorus

3. I don't have to talk out loud;
   I know You hear me.
   I don't have to be in a church;
   Don't have to be on my knees.

   Chorus

hear

know

heart

love

I love you

thank you
(like throwing a kiss)

Words and Music: Anonymous.

index by Topic

TELLING OTHERS

FAMILY RELATIONSHIPS

OBEYING GOD

Alphabetical index